Stego-cumulus

Hilary Leung

illustrated by
Niall Eccles

North Winds Press

An Imprint of Scholastic Canada Ltd.

The paintings for this book were created in ink and watercolour.

Library and Archives Canada Cataloguing in Publication

Leung, Hilary, author
Stego-cumulus / Hilary Leung ; illustrated by Niall Eccles.

ISBN 978-1-4431-5753-7 (hardcover)

1. Clouds--Juvenile literature. 2. Imagination--Juvenile
literature. 3. Friendship--Juvenile literature. I. Eccles, Niall, illustrator
II. Title.

QC921.35.L48 2018   j551.57'6   C2017-905897-5

www.scholastic.ca

6 5 4 3 2 1   Printed in Malaysia   108   18 19 20 21 22

To Anne and Daniel, who made this book possible!

— H.L.

To Mom, Dad, Ash, Brit and Sarah — thank you all.

— N.E.

Panda loved to draw, dance and play music.

Parrot enjoyed reading, building and solving puzzles.

One day, Panda wanted to dance and Parrot wanted to put the finishing touches on a castle.

But Parrot couldn't concentrate with Panda's loud music, and Panda got bored of dancing alone.

They decided to go on
a hike instead.

It was the perfect day for cloud watching.

Panda and Parrot headed to the top of their favourite hill.

From there, they could spend hours gazing at the shifting shapes and textures above.

"Look up in the sky — it's a giant dandelion," said Panda.

"That's a cirrostratus," replied Parrot.

"And there's a schooner on the sea," said Panda.

"You mean an altostratus," replied Parrot.

"Wow! A prancing Pegasus!" said Panda.

"Technically, that's a stratocumulus!" replied Parrot.

"Lonely lantern!" exclaimed Panda.

"That's a cumulonimbus!" retorted Parrot.

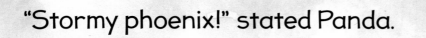
"Stormy phoenix!" stated Panda.

"Nimbostratus!" snapped Parrot.

"NO! The phoenix is right there!" shouted Panda.

"NO! The science is right there!" Parrot shouted back.

"How could Parrot not see the beautiful phoenix?" pondered Panda.

"How could Panda not see the genus of atmospheric cloud?" wondered Parrot.

Before long, the friends missed each other. Their thoughts drifted back to the skies.

"Hmmm, that altocumulus looks like tasty popcorn," said Parrot out loud.

"And that hungry mackerel could be a cirrocumulus," thought Panda.

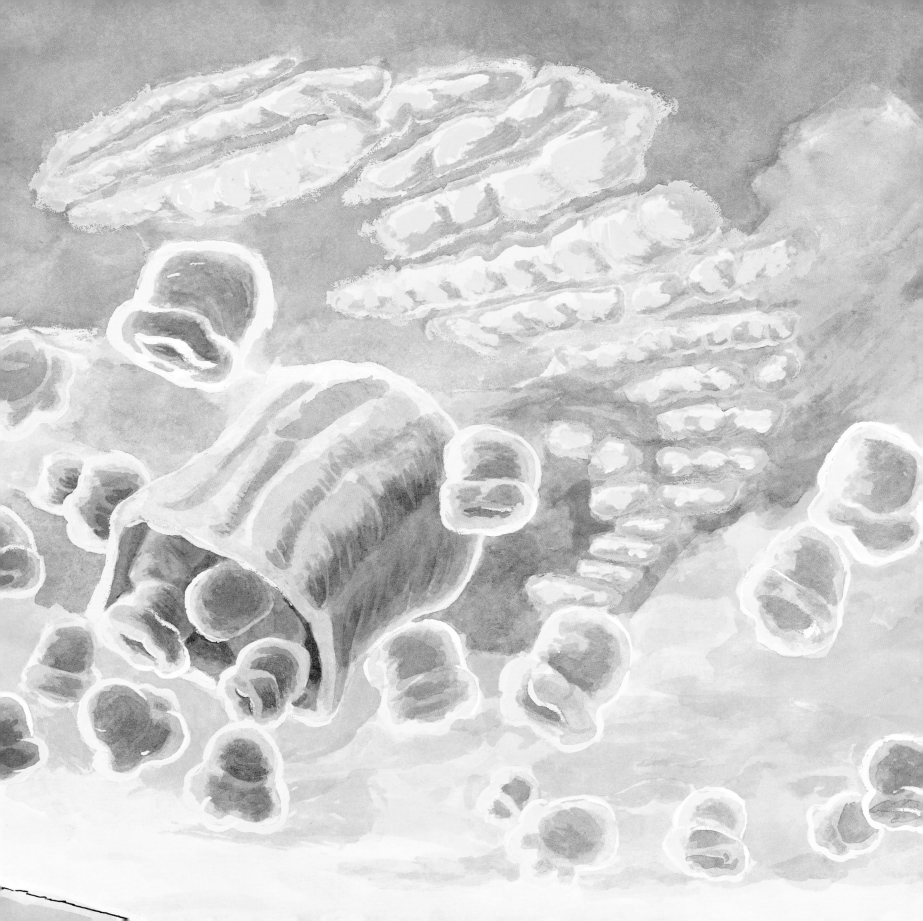

"Cirrus?" asked Panda.

"Singing sea serpent!" replied Parrot.

"Stegosaurus?" asked Parrot.

"Cumulus . . ." said Panda.

"STEGO-CUMULUS!" they exclaimed together.

The sun began to set and soon it was too dark to cloud watch. The friends smiled anyway, because tomorrow was going to be another cloudy day.

"Hey look — a shooting star!"
"That's a UFO."

Parrot's Cloud Notes

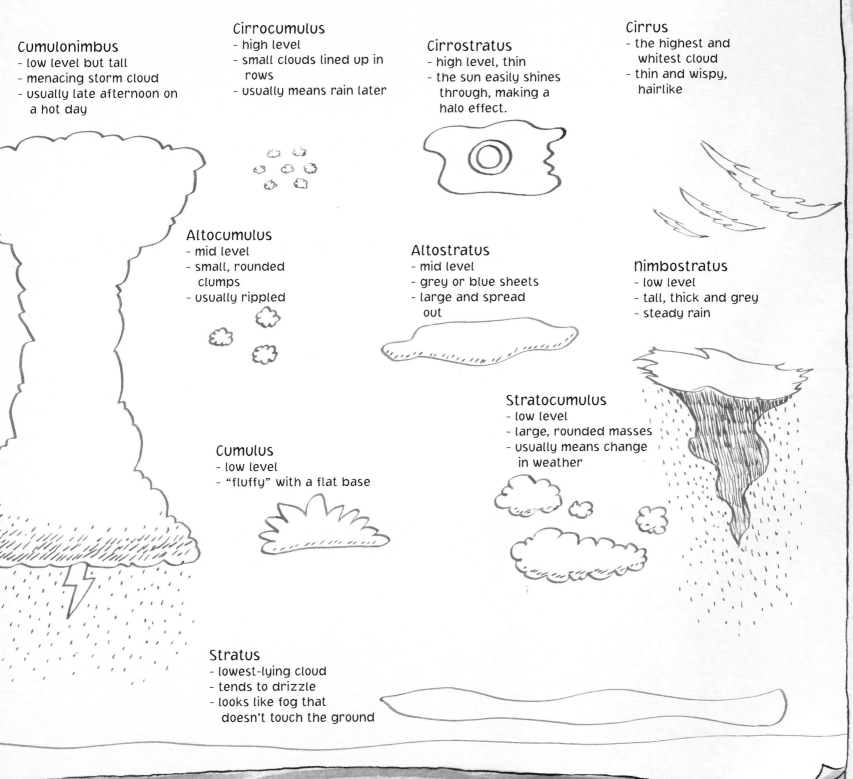

Cumulonimbus
- low level but tall
- menacing storm cloud
- usually late afternoon on a hot day

Cirrocumulus
- high level
- small clouds lined up in rows
- usually means rain later

Cirrostratus
- high level, thin
- the sun easily shines through, making a halo effect.

Cirrus
- the highest and whitest cloud
- thin and wispy, hairlike

Altocumulus
- mid level
- small, rounded clumps
- usually rippled

Altostratus
- mid level
- grey or blue sheets
- large and spread out

Nimbostratus
- low level
- tall, thick and grey
- steady rain

Stratocumulus
- low level
- large, rounded masses
- usually means change in weather

Cumulus
- low level
- "fluffy" with a flat base

Stratus
- lowest-lying cloud
- tends to drizzle
- looks like fog that doesn't touch the ground

Panda and Parrot's Cloud Notes

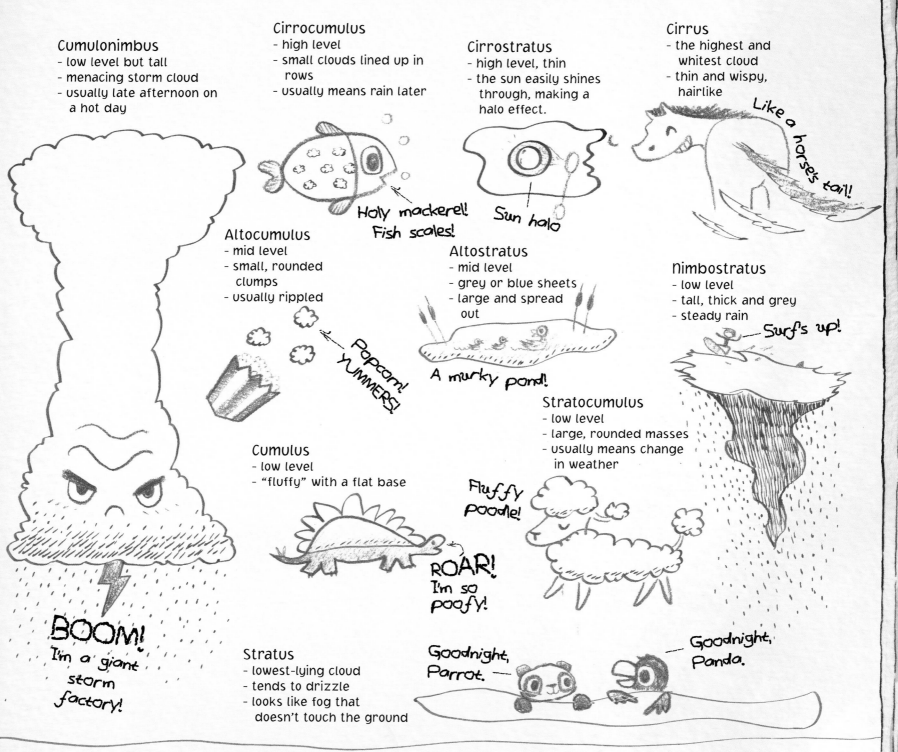

Cumulonimbus
- low level but tall
- menacing storm cloud
- usually late afternoon on a hot day

BOOM! I'm a giant storm factory!

Cirrocumulus
- high level
- small clouds lined up in rows
- usually means rain later

Holy mackerel! Fish scales!

Cirrostratus
- high level, thin
- the sun easily shines through, making a halo effect.

Sun halo

Cirrus
- the highest and whitest cloud
- thin and wispy, hairlike

Like a horse's tail!

Altocumulus
- mid level
- small, rounded clumps
- usually rippled

Popcorn! YUMMERS!

Altostratus
- mid level
- grey or blue sheets
- large and spread out

A murky pond!

Nimbostratus
- low level
- tall, thick and grey
- steady rain

Surf's up!

Cumulus
- low level
- "fluffy" with a flat base

ROAR! I'm so poofy!

Stratocumulus
- low level
- large, rounded masses
- usually means change in weather

Fluffy Poodle!

Stratus
- lowest-lying cloud
- tends to drizzle
- looks like fog that doesn't touch the ground

Goodnight, Parrot.

Goodnight, Panda.